TLCA

Traffic Light Control Agent

A Thesis

Presented for the

Master of Science

Degree

The University of Memphis

Ashraf Anwar

December 1997

ACKNOWLEDGMENTS

I would like to thank my advisor, Dr. Stan Franklin, for his continued support and advice beside his invaluable expertise in artificial intelligence which was the source of the agent part in this work. Also I would like to thank Dr. John Reece for his invaluable support regarding image processing techniques used in this work.

ABSTRACT

Research in artificial intelligence has made much progress in the eighties and nineties. However, integration of advances and achievements from various fields is still needed to reach the target of human-like intelligence and interaction. Combining mechanisms from control structures of autonomous agents with perception and image processing capabilities, TLCA is a step in that direction. TLCA is able to make use of images taken for all the directions of an intersection and process them to determine, intelligently, which direction to be green and which to be red. The aim is to avoid unnecessary green lights for directions which have no cars or vehicles coming. Future work will try to accommodate for contingencies like accidents. More research needs to be done to enhance the performance of the perception module and incorporate dynamic in-field learning.

TABLE OF CONTENTS

LIST OF FIGURES

CHAPTER 1

INTRODUCTION

Research in artificial intelligence has made much progress in the eighties and nineties. However, integration of advances and achievements from various fields is still needed to reach the target of human-like intelligence and interaction, see Bates, Loyall, and Reilly (1991, 1992). Such an integration will be mandatory, I think to, achieve the goal of Artificial Intelligence researchers all over the years, of building machines and systems possessing multiple features out of the broad range of human intelligence, see Franklin (1995), Russel and Norvig (1995), Boden (1988), Albus (1991), and Albus (1981).

1.1 AI Moving Target

One of the major difficulties in working with Artificial Intelligence is that we are chasing a moving target. This is in part due to the lack of an accurate agreed upon definition of intelligence. Whenever a task, which was previously hard to accomplish, is automated, it is no longer considered intelligent or smart, at least from many people's point of view. Also mind is based upon

Our perception capabilities enable us to extract relevant data and create useful information (percepts) out of the huge amount of sensory input obtained through our sensors. Think about the amount of data accessible through only vision. That amount of data is practically infinite, if not absolutely infinite. Nevertheless, we are able to extract a very tiny portion out of this huge unlimited amount of data, to create relevant information out of, without any considerable effort at all, if any. It is almost trivial for us. Furthermore, anyone trying to capture all of the data obtained through the visual apparatus without discarding irrelevant data, will either give up on the first or at most second attempt, or get mad! The overwhelming amount of data, absorbed by our visual apparatus, is too huge for our human weak capabilities of perception to accommodate. Moreover, if perception is that limited, cognition and consciousness are more and more limited, see Franklin (1995) and Baars (1995).

Even our memory is limited. Memory is an essential component of intelligence, see Glenberg (1996), specially short-term memory. Consider a mathematician without a memory, he or she cannot even proceed in any sort of theorem proof. Each step in the proof is based somehow on a preceding step. Even for everyday life, lack of memory will make our daily life almost impossible.

Knowing how weak our capabilities are in an absolute sense, it is amazing that *"proper"* use of such capabilities has been able to make the human race make giant steps in so many fields of knowledge. Think about all modern inventions in computers, autos, space, aviation, ... etc. You will be amazed at how good we are in *"forgetting or ignoring"* irrelevant information in order to *"focus our attention"* on what is relevant. So, to optimize one aspect, you have to not optimize at all, or even minimize or forget, about many other aspects. There is also this ever lasting challenge of the infiniteness of science. The more we know, the more we find that there were some things we were not aware of. Almost each new discovery yields another and another. So, instead of reaching the target, we find out that our target has moved further, *"the more you know, the less you know!"*

Now, here is a big issue. How can we tell a *"proper"* use of our capabilities from an improper one ? How can we determine what to pay attention to ? A lot of work has been done in this area, see Bundesen and Shibuya (1995), Foner and Maes (1994), and Callari and Ferie (1996). But no complete solution has been found so far. It is still an art not a science. I think that this is one of the major obstacles in the way of achieving human-like intelligence in a broad sense.

1.2 Autonomous Agents

I find the definition of an autonomous agent by Stan Franklin one of the most accurate definitions reflecting the broad sense of the word. According to Franklin, an autonomous agent is an agent which is situated in an environment, senses it, acts upon it overtime such that its actions may affect what the agent senses next, and its actions are in pursue of its own agenda. See Franklin (1995, 1997), Franklin and Graesser (1997), and Russel and Norvig (1995) for more detailed discussion and examples.

A cognitive agent, on the other hand, is an autonomous agent which -or who- has some of the cognitive capabilities : problem solving, planning. learning, perception, emotions, ...etc (Franklin and Graesser, 1997).

According to the above definitions, we have a broad range of autonomous agents ranging from simplest ones, e.g., a thermostat, to the most sophisticated ones, humans.

TLCA is considered to be an autonomous agent but not yet a cognitive agent.

1.3 TLCA Overview

TLCA is a traffic light control software agent. TLCA expects as input the images of the different incoming roads in an intersection - typically four-. Those images are currently recognized only if they were in (.ras) format. But, this can be overcome easily using any commercially available image processing package to convert between any other image format, e.g., gif, jpeg, tiff, ...etc., to ras format.

TLCA uses an SDM, Sparse Distributed Memory, see chapters 2, 3 for details, as a recognition memory. Images of typical cars in various positions and sizes - using rotation, scaling, translation, ...- are stored in SDM in terms of their Fourier Descriptors (see chapters 4, 5 for details). An input image of an intersection direction is supplied to the SDM as the input retrieval cue. If a match is found, that traffic direction is considered to be active, otherwise it is considered to be passive and it will have red light. Obviously, for sake of safety, no two crossing directions are green at the same time, even if one of them is passive.

Depending on whether the two perpendicular (crossing) directions are active or only one of them, TLCA will either allocate time slices of green light for both perpendicular directions or make the one active direction green and the other red, as long as no vehicles are coming in the other direction.

Some readers may wonder, why bother use autonomous agents control structures and image processing techniques, if a mechanical (push-down switch activated from a distance by incoming cars) or infra-red sensors can be used to detect the existence of incoming cars ? The answer to the above question is summarized as follows:

1- A blind sensor (mechanical or infra-red) is not able to detect contingencies, e.g., accidents or ambulance or police cars. Although not yet implemented in the current version, such enhancements can be added with moderate effort and they are among the future directions (see chapter 8, #1) to be considered.

2- TLCA has an advantage over such blind recognizers. With some extra work, TLCA will be able to estimate the number of vehicles in each direction using the same modules and control mechanisms currently in use with some additional perception modules. On the other hand, to achieve this goal with blind sensors, a group of such sensors need to be used in each direction at distant intervals.

3- Another advantage TLCA has over blind sensors, is that an image can capture an incoming car from a long distance, whereas blind sensors cannot detect such a car unless planted a long distance from the intersection.

4- One more advantage of TLCA is that it can be centralized with the traffic light itself. The entire embodiment of TLCA can be a box smaller than the physical intersection light. On the other hand, using blind sensors will require

6

implantation of sensors at regular distances which will communicate back and forth with the intersection traffic light, thus losing some of the advantages of a centralized control. In addition, extra expensive circuitry will be needed to transmit the signals from those remote blind sensors to the control circuitry governing the intersection.

One of the lessons learned from TLCA is that even for simple domains, sensation is not enough. Perception is indeed needed to achieve the goal.

This work demonstrates that SDM can serve as a control mechanism for action selection in autonomous agents.

The architecture of TLCA is depicted in *figure 1.3-1* next page.

An outline of TLCA operation is as follows:

1. The sensory input comes from cameras or whatever device yielding images in some recognizable format (currently .ras format).

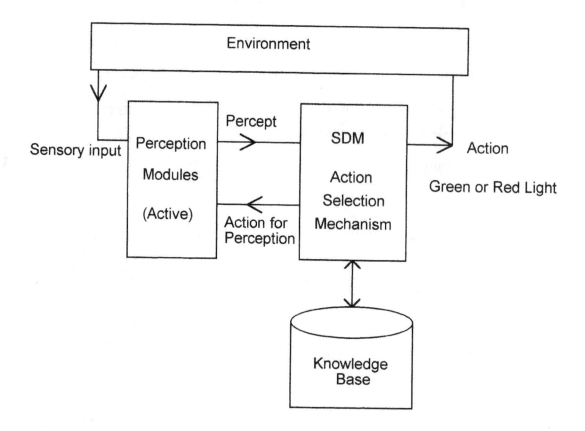

Fig 1.3-1: TLCA Overview

2. The perception modules act upon the senses to extract the percept which will carry the features or descriptors of the input image. The operation of the perception modules is discussed in detail in chapters 4 and 5.

3. The percept is supplied to the SDM, which in turn determines what action to take, depending on the existence of vehicles in each direction.

4. TLCA determines whether extra information is needed to make a decision, in which case, a signal is sent back to the perception modules asking for

8

further information which may require more sensation of the environment or reprocessing of previous senses. Otherwise, TLCA may reach a decision which means that TLCA can decide affirmatively - through the use of SDM as an action selection mechanism- about the green-red status of the intersection directions. For details about the inner workings of SDM see chapters 2 and 3.

5. The decision reached yields the action which will be carried out to reflect the state of the traffic light.

6. The knowledge base (KB) contains a group of pre-stored images of vehicles represented as Fourier Descriptors (see chapters 4 and 5). Those templates are prewritten in our SDM to form recognition patterns.

CHAPTER 2

SDM, PRINCIPLES AND ARCHITECTURE

Sparse Distributed Memory is a content-addressable memory technique invented by Pentti Kanerva, see Kanerva (1990). Some enhancements were done by the RWCP Neuro SICS Laboratory in Sweden, see Kristoferson (1995a, 1995b). Hereunder is a brief description of the ideas involved and the underlying mechanism.

The impatient reader is advised to skim through the foundations, sec 2.1. Then read 2.4 thoroughly. Section 2.7 is a possible application for SDM in agent-based environments. Finally, section 2.8 focuses on some notes.

The following sections are somehow thorough explanation about SDM, see Kanerva (1990). Some enhancements to SDM are taken from Kristoferson (1995a, 1995b), Karlsson (1995), and Sjodin (1995). Most of the figures and tables in this chapter are taken without change from "Sparse Distributed Memory", Kanerva (1990). All the SDM techniques used in this project, are due, at least in-part, to Stan Franklin.

2.1 Foundations

Sparse Distributed Memory is based on the use of a Binary Space $\{0,1\}^n$, where $N = 2^n$ stands for the space. For a string x to belong to such a space : $x \in N$ iff $x_i \in \{0,1\}$ $\forall i$. One possible way to implement such a space is to use a neuron for each physical address in the space as described in 2.1.2.

2.1.1 Binary Spaces

Some useful properties and measures for strings x, y, and z which belong to a binary space N, with n dimensions and 2^n population size, are:

1. Norm of a point x : $|x|$: number of 1's in x

2. Difference: $x-y = y-x = x \oplus y$ (n-tuple having 1 whenever x and y differ)

3. Distance: $d(x,y) = d(y,x) = |x-y|$

   $d(0,y) = |y-0| = |y|$, where 0 is the zero string (all zeros)

4. Betweenness: a point y is said to be between x and z, x:y:z, if

   $d(x,z)=d(x,y)+d(y,z)$.

   For a set Y, x:Y:z if $\forall$ y $\in$ Y, x:y:z

11

Betweenness is symmetric but not transitive. Note that the whole space N is between a point and its complement, i.e., x:N:x`.

5. Orthogonality (indifference): (exact only for n even)

$$x \perp y \text{ iff } d(x,y) = n/2 \quad \text{(indifference distance)}$$

$$x \perp y ==> x \perp y`, \text{ where } y` \text{ is the complement of } y$$

6. Circle O(r,x) : set of points at most r bits from x

$$O(r,x) = \{ y| d(x,y) <= r\}$$

$$O(n,x) = N$$

7. The Distribution of Space N:

Number of points exactly d points from given point x (origin) = $\binom{n}{d}$

{number of ways to choose d coordinates from a total of n}

N ~ binomial(n, 0.5)   { n Bernoulli Trials }

mean = np = n/2

variance = np(1-p) = n/4

$$N(d) = \Pr\{d(x,y) <= d\}$$

$$\cong F\{(d-n/2)/(\sqrt{n}/2)\} \quad \text{[normal approximation to binomial]}$$

{Normal Distribution. : $E(x) = n/2$, $\sigma_x = \sqrt{n}/2$}

8. Tendency to orthogonality:

Most of the space lies at approximately the mean distance n/2 from a point which is a characteristic of the normal distribution. Also, Over 0.999999 of the space lies within five times the standard deviation (σ) of the mean. For the case of n=1000, the following calculations hold:

$$n=1000, \quad \bar{x} = 500, \quad \sigma_x = \sqrt{n}/2 = 15.8$$

About 99.999% of the space lies within $500 \pm 5*15.8$, i.e. lies in the range [422, 578] bits from a specific point.

9. Distribution of the Circle O(r,x) :

$$\text{circle area} \quad = N * N(r)$$
$$\cong N * F\{(r - n/2) / \sqrt{n}/2 \}$$

r_p = radius of circle that encloses p of the space N

$N(r_p) = p$

$|O(r_p,x)| = pN$

Table 2.1.1-1 next page, gives the radii r_p of x-centered circles of N that encloses specified portions of the space N.

Note that in order to include any considerable portion of the space, r_p must be sufficiently close to n/2, and then when r_p exceeds n/2 slightly, almost all space is included. So, Only 10^{-9} of the space lies within 405 bit distance. Thus, we can obtain mostly correct match with such difference in cue.

Table 2.1.1-1 : *Radii* r_p *of x-centered circles of N that encloses specified portions of the space N.*

portion p of the space N within rp bits of point x	Number of s, n = 100		n = 1,000		n = 10,000	
	rp Bits	% of n	rp Bits	% of n	Rp Bits	% of n
0.000000001	20	20	405	41	4700	47
0.00000001	22	22	411	41	4720	47.2
0.0000001	24	24	418	42	4740	47.4
0.000001	26	26	425	42	4760	47.6
0.00001	29	29	433	43	4790	47.9
0.0001	31	31	441	44	4810	48.1
0.0005	34	34	448	45	4840	48.4
0.001	35	35	451	45	4850	48.5
0.01	38	38	463	46	4880	48.8
0.1	44	44	480	48	4940	49.4
0.25	47	47	489	49	4970	49.7
0.5	50	50	500	50	5000	50

Source: Kanerva (1990)

2.1.2 Content-Addressable vs. Associative

Content addressable memory is usually more expensive than ordinary memory since each location contains circuits (address decoder) needed to determine whether there exist a match or not (e.g. n-way associative -using computer terminology- memory).

According to Kanerva, we can convert ordinary memory into content addressable by : 1. assigning first k bits of each location to hold the address

2. making sure when writing that no two words have the same first k bits.

14

Thus it becomes a 1:1 mapping, which means that selection becomes unique as in conventional RAM. Whereas in true content addressable, selection need not be unique.

In SDM, many locations are selected (shared) by same address. Selection is based on whether the location address is similar to retrieval cue, rather than part of location contents match the cue.

2.1.3 One Possible Memory Implementation

Each physical address can be implemented using a neuron. The address lines of each neuron correspond to the cell binary address. Thus, the number of address lines is equal to the size of each stored binary word.

The address, a, of a neuron with input coefficients w_i $i=0,1,...,n-1$ is defined as the n-bit input pattern that maximizes the weighted sum. The maximum occurs when inhibitory inputs are zeros and excitatory inputs are ones:

$$a_i = \begin{array}{llll} 1 & \quad \text{if } w_i > 0 & \quad \text{excitatory} \\ 0 & \quad \text{if } w_i < 0 & \quad \text{inhibitory} \end{array}$$

If $w_i = 0$, then that neuron output is independent from this input and it could be removed.

The maximum weighted sum S(w) is the sum of positive coefficients.

The point opposite to the neuron's address, a`, gives the minimum weighted sum s(w) which is the sum of negative coefficients.

When the threshold c of a neuron is in the range $s < c \leq S$, the neuron output is 0 for some addresses (input patterns) and 1 for others, as follows:

1. If $c > S$, the output of the neuron is always 0.

2. If $c \leq s$, the neuron output is always 1.

3. if $c = S$, the neuron responds only to its own address and acts like an address decoder of a conventional RAM (unique selection).

4. If $c = S - d$, the neuron responds to all the addresses that are within d bits of the neuron's address, a. These addresses form a region around a , called the <u>response region</u> of the neuron with point a at the center of the region and the response region size is equal to $O(d,a) = N*N(d)$.

2.2 The Best Match Machine

The 'Best Match Machine' is a content addressable memory with $N = 2^n$ locations. It is *not* Kanerva's final memory model. Rather, it is used to illustrate the problem of best match. Each location has the capacity of one n-bit storage. Address decoding is done by N address decoder neurons.

The effective threshold of neuron x is equal to $|x| - d$, where $|x|$ is the maximum weighted sum, and d is a common parameter for the whole memory to adjust all thresholds when accessing the memory. So, location x is accessible every time the address x is within d bits of the address presented to the memory.

Assume that each location has a special location-occupied bit that can be accessed in the same way as the regular data bits. Writing a word to a location sets the location-occupied bit. We can read occupied locations only.

Initially, mark the whole memory as unoccupied by setting $d = n$ and execute *clear location-occupied bit* command.

Set $d = 0$. Write each word ϕ of the data set at address ϕ (Content Addressable).

To find the best match for a word z, place z in the address register, then find the least distance d for which there exists an occupied location.

17

Some of the drawbacks of the 'Best Match Machine' are :

1. Not all 2^n locations are occupied. Unoccupied locations need not be implemented (no need for address decoder). Which calls for the use of the second model, *Sparse* Memory.

2. It is not suitable for sequences storage and retrieval.

2.3 Sparse Memory

It is not practical to construct best match machine with memory that has 2^{1000} physical storage locations. Even 2^{100} water molecules will more than fill the human brain. Also, the number of neurons in the nervous system is about 2^{36}. With such a vast address space, *most* of the addresses cannot be represented by an address decoder and a storage location. Furthermore, there is no need to use 2^{1000} storage locations, since a human lifetime is too short to store anywhere near 2^{1000} independent entities (a century has fewer than 2^{32} seconds).

2.3.1 How it Works

A word can be stored in memory by writing it in a free location and at the same time providing the location with the appropriate address decoder. The storage locations and their addresses are given from the start, and only the contents of the locations are modifiable. The storage locations are very few

18

with respect to 2^n (i.e. sparse memory). They are distributed randomly in the $\{0,1\}^n$ address spaces.

Neurons (linear threshold functions) are used for address decoding. An address-decoder neuron with fixed input synapses could function as a storage location.

The addresses of the locations N ` of a sparse memory are a uniform random sample of the address space N. N' will be called set of <u>hard locations</u> to emphasize that they are physical locations.

The distance between locations means distance between corresponding addresses.

Nearest N'-neighbor x' to an element (address) x of N, is the most similar element of N' to x. If $X \subset N$, then $X' \subset N'$ is the set of the nearest N'-neighbors of elements of X :

$$X' = \{ x' | x \in X \}$$

Distance of the nearest location $d(x,x')$:

$$N(d) = \Pr\{ d(x,y) \le d \}, \text{ for arbitrary points x and y}$$
$$N'(d) = \Pr\{ d(x,x') \le d \}$$
$$= 1 - [1 - N(d)]^{N'}$$

19

$$= 1 - [\, 1 - N' * N(d) \,/\, N' \,]^{N'}$$

$$\cong 1 - e^{-N' * N(d)},$$

the approximation is excellent when N' is large and $N(d)$ is small ($N' > 1000$, $N(d) < 1/N'$).

When $N(d) = 1/N'$:

$$N'(d) \cong 1 - e^{-1} = 0.63$$

This means that :

Pr{a circle size of $1/N'$ of N contains at least 1 hard location} $= 0.63$

$$N(d) \cong -\ln[\, 1 - N'(d)\,] \,/\, N' \quad , \text{ which implies that}$$

$$d \cong N^{-1}[\, -\ln(1 - N'(d)) \,/\, N'\,]$$

The median of the distance $d(x,x') = N^{-1}[\, -\ln(0.5) \,/\, N'\,]$

From table 2.3.1-1 below : the median $= 423.7 \cong 424$

That median is a good measure for the distance between a random point of N and the hard location nearest to it.

Table 2.3.1-1 : *Distribution of distance to nearest storage location, N`(d), in a 1,000-dimensional memory with 1,000,000 locations.*

d	N`(d)	z	N(d)
388.8	0.000001	-7.03	1E-12
394	0.00001	-6.71	1E-11
399.4	0.0001	-6.36	1E-10
405.2	0.001	-6	0.000000001
411.3	0.01	-5.61	0.00000001
417.9	0.1	-5.19	0.0000001
421	0.25	-5	0.0000003
423.7	0.5	-4.83	0.0000007
425.9	0.75	-4.69	0.000001
427.6	0.9	-4.58	0.000002
429.9	0.99	-4.43	0.000005
431.3	0.999	-4.35	0.000007
432.2	0.9999	-4.28	0.000009
433.1	0.99999	-4.23	0.000012
433.7	0.999999	-4.19	0.000014

z is the number of standard deviations that d is below the mean distance 500 :

z= (d - 500) /15.8

N(d) is the distribution of the space N : N(d) = Pr{d(x,y) <= d} = F(z)

Source: Kanerva (1990)

2.3.2 The nearest neighbor method

X is random set of 10,000 words of $\{0,1\}^{1000}$. There are 10^6 hard locations to store X in. The goal is to find the stored word that matches a test word the best. We store each word ζ of X in its nearest hard location ζ'.

However, to find the best match to a test word z , if we read the nearest occupied hard location z', it would not, in general, contain the best match or even probably a good match.

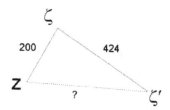

Fig 2.3.2-1 : The distance from z to the location ζ', where the best-matching word ζ is stored. The "unknown" distance $d(z, \zeta')$ is approximately 454 bits.

For example, *See figure 2.3.2-1 above*, z is a test word. ζ is the element of X most similar to z. $d(z , \zeta) = 200$ (i.e. they are quite similar). Assume that $d(\zeta , \zeta') = 424$ (median distance). Then using the third side of a triangle rule, $d(z , \zeta') \cong a + b - 2*A*b / n = 454$ bits. Using *table 2.1.1-1* , about 0.0017 N′ $= 1700$ hard locations, are within 454 bits of z. About 10^{-2} of them (17) locations are occupied by elements of X. Hence,

$$\Pr \{ \text{ nearest X'-neighbor of } z = \zeta' \mid d(z , \zeta) = 200 \} \cong 1/17$$

It can be shown using the third side of a triangle rule that two dissimilar addresses u , v can refer to the same hard location, i.e., $u' = v'$

Things become worse when data other than the addresses themselves are stored in memory ($<\zeta,\eta>$ instead of $<\zeta,\zeta>$). The probability of success in our example is 1/17. We cannot even tell, by reading from memory, whether the outcome is a success or failure (which corresponds psychologically to knowing whether one knows).

2.4 Sparse Distributed Memory

Many Storage locations participate in a single write or read operation. So, data will be retrieved on the basis of similarity of address. If $<\zeta,\eta>$ is a stored address-data pair then reading from an address x that is sufficiently similar to ζ retrieves a word y that is even more similar to η than x is to ζ. The similarities are comparable since the address to memory and the data are elements of the same metric space N.

2.4.1 How it Works

The storage locations and their addresses are given from the start, and only the contents are modifiable. The threshold of the address decoders can even be fixed.

Access Circle, O′(x), is the set of hard locations $O'(r,x)$ in the circle $O(r,x)$. In this notation we are omitting the access radius r which is fixed to the permissible distance range of contributing (accessible) locations in Read/Write operations. Note that $O'(x) = N' \cap O(x)$.

23

For example, if r = 0.001, then 0.001 of N (and 0.001 of N' on the average) is accessed at once. From *table 2.1.1-1*, a circle of radius of 451 bits covers 0.001 of the space, and so the access radius $r_{0.001} = 451$ bits.

Most locations in the access circle are quite far from the center. The location closest to the center is 424 bits on the average (median distance, see *table 2.3.1-1*).

The average distance from the center to the 1000 locations of the access circle is 448 bits (from *table 2.1.1-1*, a circle with 448-bit radius encloses 0.001 / 2= 0.0005 of the space) which is only three bits short of the maximum distance.

Access Overlap, I'(x,y), is the set of hard locations accessible from both x and y, I'(x,y) = O'(x) ∩ O'(y). The mean number of hard locations in this access overlap depends on :

        1- size of access circle

        2- distance d(x,y) between the centers

See table 2.4.1-1 next page.

Content of a location, C(x'), is a multiset of all the words that have ever been written to it, mapped somehow. *Writing in x'* means adding the written word, η, to the multiset of words C(x') contained in x', C(x') = C(x') ψ [η].

Writing word η at ξ means writing η in all the (1000) hard locations accessible from ξ.

Data at x, D(x), is the pooled contents (multiunion) of all locations accessible from x, $D(x) = \psi\ C(y')$, $y' \in O'(x)$.

Table 2.4.1-1 : Mean number of hard locations in access overlap of two circles with radii $r_{0.001} = 451$ *in a 1,000-dimensional memory with 1,000,000 locations.*
d is the distance, in bits, between the centers of the two circles.

d	Number of location	d	Number of location	d	Number of location	d	Number of location	d	Number of location
0	1000	21	619	60	400	160	146	360	13
1	894	23	603	65	376	170	132	370	11
2	894	25	588	70	361	180	119	380	10
3	842	27	573	75	339	190	107	390	8
4	842	29	559	80	326	200	97	400	7
5	803	31	546	85	307	210	87	410	6
6	803	33	533	90	295	220	78	420	5
7	770	35	521	95	277	230	70	430	4
8	770	37	509	100	267	240	62	440	4
9	743	39	497	105	251	250	55	450	3
10	743	41	486	110	241	260	49	460	2
11	718	43	475	115	228	270	44	470	2
12	718	45	465	120	219	280	39	480	2
13	695	47	455	125	206	290	34	490	1
14	695	49	445	130	198	300	30	500	1
15	674	51	435	135	186	310	26	510	1
16	674	53	426	140	179	320	23	520	1
17	655	55	417	145	169	330	20	530	0
18	655	57	408	150	162	340	18	540	0
19	636	59	400	155	152	350	15	550	0

Source: Kanerva (1990)

If the word η has been written with the address ξ, the multiset $D(x)$ -when reading at x- contains $|O'(x) \cap O'(\xi)|$ copies of η, one from each location accessible from both x and ξ.

Reading at x means taking a representative (element of N) of the data at x. *Word at x, W(x)* is a properly chosen representative of $D(x)$.

Finding the best match requires :

1-not too many words have been stored : sparse
2-the first reading address (test pattern) is sufficiently close to the writing address of the target word.

Storing the entire data set (10^4) each in 1000 locations, means that some 10^7 words are stored in memory. This gives our first estimate for the capacity of a storage location which is 10 words per location.

Reading will pool the data of about 1000 locations, yielding a multiset $D(x)$ of about 10,000 words.

$$|X| = 10,000$$
$$|O'(x)| \cong 1000$$
$$|C(x')| \cong 10$$
$$|D(x)| \cong 10,000$$
$$C(x') = X \cap O(x')$$

A representative of the pooled data D(z) - when reading at test word z - is obtained by computing an element of N that is an archetype of the pooled data D(z) but not necessarily an element of it. We will take the average of the words of D(z) (majority rule) . This average is the best representative of D(z) in the sense that it is the word of N with the smallest mean distance to the words of D(z). The ith bit of the average is given by summing over the ith bits of the words in the pooled data and then thresholding with half the size of the pooled data: $W_i(z) = 1$ iff $\Sigma \xi_i \geq |D(z)| / 2$, $\xi \in D(z)$. That representative is a good one as long as the words written in memory are a random sample of N.

2.4.2 Convergence to the Best-Matching Word

When we read at ξ, if we have previously written the word ξ at ξ, we retrieve 1000 copies of ξ in addition to about 10,000 copies of other words for a total of 11,000 (10,000 if reading at a random address). However, the other words come mostly in ones or in very small groups, since the intersection of the read circle $O'(\xi)$ with the write circle $O'(x)$, for most x in N and in X, is about 0.001 of $O'(\xi)$, or just one hard location. Against such *background noise*, the weight of 1,000 is sufficient for the retrieval (reconstruction) of ξ.

Pr { guessing 1 bit correctly } $\cong 1 - 10^{-22}$

Pr { guessing all 1000 bits correctly } $\cong (1 - 10^{-22})^{1000} \cong 1 - 10^{-19}$

Thus, we are nearly certain that $W(\xi) = \xi$

When we read starting from test word z, the new distance to the target $d(W(z), \xi)$ depends on the old distance, $d(z, \xi)$. *See figure 2.4.2-1 next page.* Iterated reading fails to converge to the best-matching word if the original distance, $d(z, \xi)$, is too large. In our example, a test word more than 209 bits (critical distance) from the target will not, in general, find its target. The reading sequence will diverge until it becomes near 500 (indifference distance). *See figure 2.4.2-2 next page.*

Chance convergence might happen if an initially diverging sequence converge to a random word of the data set X. This is characterized by a very long expected time to convergence. Expected time of *chance convergence* is extremely long. In our example, the probability that a random point of N is within the critical distance of 209 bits of the nearest point of X is something like 10^{-50}, and so the expected time of chance convergence to some point of X is about 10^{50} iterations.

Critical Distance is the distance beyond which divergence is more likely than convergence (209 bits in our example). As more words are stored in memory, the critical distance decreases until it reaches zero, and thereafter it vanishes, meaning that stored words are no longer retrievable, i.e. there is no convergence anywhere.

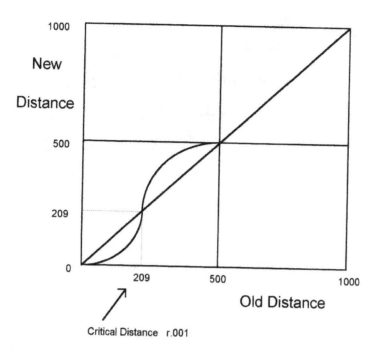

Fig 2.4.2-1 : New distance to target as a function of old distance

Source: Kanerva (1990)

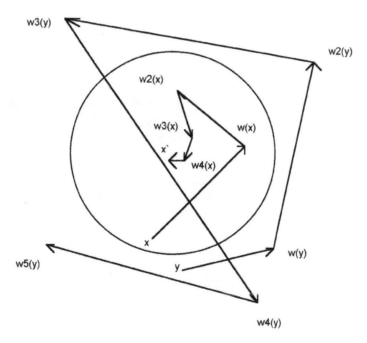

Fig 2.4.2-2 : Converging sequence (x --> x`), and diverging sequence y --> ?

Source: Kanerva (1990)

29

Rates of convergence and divergence decrease as we get closer to the critical distance. When we are sufficiently far from the critical distance, convergence to the target or divergence to random indifferent points is rapid (fewer than ten iterations, as a rule). The comparison of adjacent items of a sequence soon reveals whether the sequence will converge or (initially) diverge.

Memory Capacity T is the size of the data set for which the critical distance is zero.

$$T = N' / H(n)$$

where $H(n) = [F^{-1} (1/ 2^{1/n})]^2$

For $n = 1000$, $\qquad H(n) = 10.22 \cong 10$

Hence, $T = N' / 10$ (one-tenth of the number of hard locations)
See Table 2.4.2-1 below.

Table 2.4.2-1 : Capacity of sparse distributed memory with N' storage locations.

n (number of dimensions)	c(capacity as a multiple of N')	1/c
100	0.165	6.1
200	0.137	7.3
500	0.112	9.0
1000	0.098	10.2
2000	0.087	11.5
5000	0.076	13.2
10000	0.069	14.5
20000	0.063	15.8
50000	0.057	17.6
100000	0.053	18.9

Source: Kanerva (1990)

Full memory is a memory filled to capacity. When writing word ξ in a full memory, the probability of reading ξ at ξ is, by definition, 0.5. *Overloaded Memory* is a memory filled beyond capacity. When writing word ξ in an overloaded memory, the probability of reading ξ at ξ is less than 0.5. *In both full and overloaded memories*, the probability of reading ξ from a point only one bit far is quite small (words forgotten because of increased noise), and a sequence of successively read words diverges rapidly.

Capacity of a storage location can be calculated as follows :

Total number of words in memory

= average number of points stored in each hard loc. * number of hard loc.

= $(T * p) * N'$, where access radius is r_p

Average number of words per location (Capacity) = $T * p = (N' / 10) * p$

= 100 words (p= 0.001)

Since the average word of the pooled data can be computed from n-bit sums, a bit location can be realized as a <u>counter</u> that is incremented by 1 to store 1 and decremented by 1 to store 0. A bit location that can store the integers [-50,50] will suffice. The range of the values can be reduced to perhaps as little as [-10,10] by :

1- reducing the size of the write circle

2- not attempting to fill the memory to its capacity

31

After writing word ξ, each subsequent writing near ξ will modify some of the 1000 copies of ξ. A location survives one write operation with probability $q = 1 - p = 1 - 0.001 = 0.999$. Hence,

Pr { a location survives L write operations } = q^L

2.4.3 Some Psychological Aspects

Indication of *knowing that one knows* is indicated by fast convergence of read operations.

Tip-of-the-tongue state corresponds to being about the critical distance (slow rate of convergence).

Rehearsal is done by writing an item many times in memory.

A full or overloaded memory could support momentary feelings of familiarity that would fade away rapidly, as if *one could not maintain attention.*

2.5 Sparse Distributed Memory Construction

Addressing : The memory will be built of addressable storage locations. A location is activated whenever a read or write address is within a certain number of bits of the location's address.

Storage : A storage location has n counters, one for every bit.

Writing : To write 1 in a bit means to increment the counter. To write 0 in a bit means to decrement the counter or to do nothing.

Reading : Retrieval is done by pooling the contents of the storage locations activated by the read address, and then finding for every bit whether zeros or ones are in the majority.

Address Decoding : A storage location should be accessible from anywhere within r_p bits of the location's address. Then, the linear threshold neurons can be used for address decoding. The threshold for every address-decoder neuron would be fixed to r_p units below the decoder address (maximum weighted sum), i.e. $S - r_p$.

In computing the *average word*, the pooled bit sums are compared with a certain threshold which is the mean bit sum (add 1 for one and -1 for zero) over all the data stored in memory if writing 0 is decrementing the counter, or the mean count of ones over all the data stored in memory if writing 0 is doing nothing.

Each bit location should have 3 lines : address-decoder selection (in), write (in), and read (out).

Since many bit locations are pooled to form a single output bit from memory, they must be connected to a common output line.

Writing the data corresponds to using a matching network that takes one input line and distributes it to the same bit locations that are pooled for a single output bit.

We can use the same wire for both input and output. Alternatively, we can use matched pair of separate corresponding input and output lines.

2.6 Autonomous Learning System Organization

Our autonomous learning agent will function independently, interact with its environment and record its interaction to have the potential for learning and adaptation. It will use sparse distributed memory.

Binary vectors will stand for patterns of binary features. The mathematics generalize to patterns of multivalued features. The most important thing is that, the number of features must be large.

A pattern can be used both as an address and as a datum, a sequence of patterns can be stored as a pointer chain.

Addressing the memory need not be exact. The address patterns that have been used as write addresses *attract*, meaning that reading within the critical distance of such an address retrieves a pattern that is *closer* to the written pattern than the read address is to the write address. Three to six iterations will usually suffice to retrieve original patterns.

When similar patterns (an object viewed from different angles and distances) have been used as write addresses, the individual patterns written with those addresses cannot be recovered exactly. What is recovered, instead, is a statistical average (abstraction) of the patterns written in that neighborhood of addresses. The object is considered to occupy a region of the pattern space with poorly defined boundaries (concept).

2.6.1 Modeling the World

Many things appear to be learned by nothing more than repeated exposure to them (learn from experience). Learning is model building. We build an internal model of the world and then operate with the model. That modeling is so basic to our nature that we are hardly aware of it.

The modeling mechanism constructs objects and individuals. A person is constantly changing and our view of him are different at different times, yet we perceive him as "that person".

Operating with the model is like operating with a scale model. The model mimics actions and interactions of objects and individuals. The more experience we have, the more faithfully are the dynamics of the world reproduced by the model.

The model simply captures statistical regularities of the world, as mediated by the senses, and is able to reproduce them later. Our world model includes ourselves as a part. We can prepare ourselves for a situation by imagining ourselves in the situation.

Subjective experience produced by the outside world is of the same quality as that produced by the internal model of the world. Our internal and external "pictures" merge without our being aware of it. We scan our surroundings for overall cues and *fill in much of the detail* from the internal model. However, when something unusual happens, we begin to pay attention. We are altered by the discrepancy between the external report of what is happening and the internal report of what *should* be happening on the basis of the past experience. Moreover, the *internal* model affects our *perception* profoundly, without our being aware of it (prejudgments).

2.6.2 Storing the World Model in SDM

At any given moment, the individual is in some subjective mental state. A flow of these states (sequence) describes the individual's subjective experience over time. The state space for the world is immense in comparison with that for an individual's experience.

Individual's sensory information at a moment is represented as a long vector of features. A sequence of such vectors represent the passage of time.

Since information supplied by the senses and information supplied by the memory can produce the *same subjective experience*, they are both fed into some common part of the architecture, the *focus*.

Sequence of patterns in the focus represents the system's subjective experience about the world over time *(See figure 2.6.2-1)*.

Since sequences are stored as pointer chains, the patterns of a sequence are used both as addresses and as data, i.e., *Focus = MAR + MDR.*

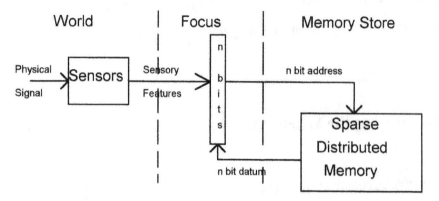

Fig 2.6.2-1 : Senses, Memory, and Focus in SDM

Source: Kanerva (1990)

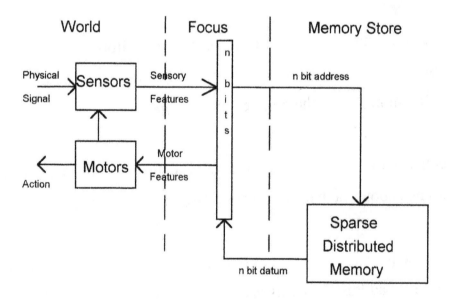

Fig 2.6.3-1 : Organization of an autonomous system using SDM

Source: Kanerva (1990)

The world model is updated by writing into the memory as follows :

1. The pattern held in the focus at time t is used to address the memory, activating a set of memory locations.

2. The response read from those locations is the memory prediction of the sensory input at time t+1.

3. If the prediction agrees with the sensory input, there is no need to adjust the memory, and the read pattern simply becomes the contents of the focus at time t+1.

4. If the prediction disagrees with the sensory input, a third correct pattern is computed from them (average) and it becomes the contents of the focus at time t+1. However, before it is used to address the memory at time t+1 , it is written in the locations from which the faulty output was just read (the locations selected at time t).

As the correction patterns are written into memory over time, the memory builds a better and better model of the world, constrained only by the senses ability to discriminate and the memory capacity to store information.

2.6.3 Including Action in the World Model

The system needs to act and learn from its interaction with the world. To act, the system needs motors (effectors). To learn, the system must *model* its own actions.

Learning to perform actions means learning to reproduce sequences of patterns that drive the muscles. Thus, the system's own actions can be included in the world model by storing motor sequences in memory in addition to sensory sequences.

Since the way in and out of the memory is through the focus, the system motors should be driven from the focus.

As the system's subjective experience is based on the information in the focus, deliberate action becomes part of the system's subjective experience without the need for additional mechanisms *(See figure 2.6.3-1 page 38)*.

Some components of the focus (50-80%) correspond to and can be controlled by the system sensors. Others (10-20%) drive the system motors. The focus could have components with no immediate external significance (status and preference function). All components of the focus can be controlled by the memory.

Retrieving well-behaved sequences from the memory to the motor part of the focus would cause the corresponding actions to be executed by the system.

2.6.4 Cued Behavior

Assume that 80% of the focus is for sensory input and 20% for motor output. Assume that the stimulus sequence <A,B,C> is to elicit the response sequence <X,Y,Z>, with A triggering action X after one time step and so on.

The pattern sequence that needs to be generated in the focus is <Aw, BX, CY, dZ> . In each pair, the first letter stands for sensory-input section and the second for motor-output section of the focus.

If <AW, BX, CY, DZ> has been written in memory, and A is presented to the focus through the senses, then BX is likely to be retrieved from the memory into the focus
$(d(Aw, AW) \leq 0.2 \, n \leq$ critical distance 209, for $n = 1000)$.

This means that action X will be performed at the time at which B is expected (predicted) to be observed.

Now, if the sensory report agrees with B, then BX will be used as the next memory address and CY will be retrieved, causing action Y, and so on if agreement persists.

If A controls significantly less than 80% of the focus, or if the cue is not exactly A but a similar pattern A', then we may not be sufficiently close to the original write address AW to retrieve BX or something similar to it. To read BX, it is then important that the action part w be similar to W.

Now, if W means that the system is *paying attention* and is waiting for a cue, and w means that the system is performing some other action. AW or A'W will retrieve BX (the system was waiting for the cue). But, Aw or A'w will not (the system was not waiting). This means that the system will respond properly to a cue only if it is waiting for the cue, i.e. the response depends on the state at the time the cue is presented.

If after BX has been read from memory, the senses input is suppressed, the focus will be controlled *entirely* by the memory, and the rest of the sequence will be recalled and the actions will be completed. But, if the agent senses feed the sequence <A,B,K,L> where K and L are quite different from C and D (sudden change), then BX will retrieve CY -action Y is executed (inertia)- and senses report K instead of C which was expected to be sensed. The next contents of the focus will be HY instead of CY (H is some combination of C and K that, in general, is quite different from C). Thus DZ will not be retrieved (failure of action Z). This failure can be explained as follows:

1. an environment monitoring system ceases to act when the proper cues are no longer present.

42

2. a system that monitors its own actions effects, stops acting when the effects no longer confirm the system expectations.

Since the pattern retrieved from the memory includes an expectation of the action results, the memory can be used to *plan actions* .

The system will initiate the "thought" in the focus and then block off the present (ignore environmental cues and suppress action execution). The memory will then retrieve into the focus the likely consequences of the contemplated actions.

2.6.5 Learning to Act

The model goodness is judged by how well it predicts the world. When the model predicts incorrectly, it is adjusted. Action correction is much harder than sensory correction. There is no *external* source feeding correct action sequences into the focus.

The action sequences have to be generated internally. They have to be evaluated as to their desirability and should be stored in memory in a way that makes desirable actions likely to be carried out and undesirable actions likely to be avoided.

2.6.5.1 Initial Conditions for Learning

We are born with built in preferences (food satisfaction) and dislikes (hot, pain) and instinctive ways to act (automatic reflexes). The learning for such actions is passed to the individual as a part of the individual's genetic endowment. Given such preferences (desirable states) and dislikes (undesirable states), we can define desirable and undesirable actions according to the states to which they lead. Some patterns in the focus (states) are inherently good or bad with most states being indifferent.

Learning to act means that the system will store in memory sequences of actions in a way that increases the likelihood of finding good states and of avoiding bad ones.

The system has a scalar preference function to evaluate patterns or subjective states (indirectly evaluate action sequences). The good states have high (positive) preference function values, and the bad states have low (negative) ones, hence the problem becomes an *optimization problem.*

Indifferent states acquire values according to whether they are found on paths to desirable or undesirable states. Thus, learning to act can be looked at as assigning preferences to states that *start out as indifferent states.*

2.6.5.2 Realizing the Preference Function

Each memory location will have a counter for the preference function. The counter value is :

  positive for good (desirable) patterns

  negative for bad (undesirable) patterns

  close to zero for indifferent or as yet undefined patterns.

On reading, counters for the preference fn. can be pooled in the same way as pattern component counters. The sum is :

  positive if favorable focus pattern

  negative if unfavorable focus pattern

  zero if indifferent focus pattern.

Built-in preference function means that some locations have nonzero function counters from the start, and that such nonzero counters may even be unmodifiable.

2.6.5.3 Trial and Error Learning

We assume that the system can block off external input after accepting the initial input (the present situation) and that it can suspend the execution of actions until it has accepted some proposed action sequence.

If the present situation strongly resembles a past one, the system will propose an action by recalling memory. Otherwise, it will _try_ a random action.

If the state reached after iterating is undesirable, then we have an _error_, and the system will try another action (backtracking). If the state reached is good, the system has reason to proceed with the proposed action.

Trial and error is reasonable if the number of situations and actions (the system state space) is small and simple, or if the proportion of desirable states is large.

The efficiency of searching and learning can be improved considerably if good paths are remembered and are used later to find inherently good states.

If an action sequence leads to a desirable pattern in the system focus, the positive preference is extended backward with decreasing intensity (as bucket brigade in Holland's classifier systems). Similarly, negative preference is extended for bad states.

2.6.5.4 Supervised Learning

Supervised learning substitutes an artificial (new) stimulus for a natural (old) one. The system already has a natural (old) response for the old stimulus and it has no response for the new stimulus.

The *trainer* presents a new stimulus (e.g., a bell) followed by an old one (food) and the system responds.

After sufficient repetition, the new stimulus *alone* will elicit the old response due to *extending the preference*.

Usually no learning occurs if the old stimulus is presented before the new one. The new stimulus can even take the place of the old stimulus in training another artificial stimulus for the old response.

2.6.5.5 Learning by Imitation

The system will use itself to model the behavior of other systems. The system must store an image of the behavior of others. It maps this image into actions of its own.

The system must observe the results of its own actions and compare them against its image of the behavior of others (i.e., the system must identify with the *role model*)

An internal reward mechanism -used to perfect the match between the system own behavior and that of the *role model*- is usually necessary if a system is going to learn by imitation, which, in turn, is primarily responsible for complicated social learning.

2.6.6 The Encoding Problem

The raw signal arriving at the sense organs is ill suited for building a predictive model. Even if a number of regularities of the world are present in the signal, they appear in far-from-optimal form and are embedded in noise.

A sensory system has two functions :

1. to filter out noise
2. to transform relevant information into a form that is useful in building and using the world model (*encoding problem*).

Since patterns stored in memory attract similar patterns, the memory chunks things with similar encodings, forming objects and individuals from them.

A sensory system must express the sensory input in features that are relatively *insensitive to scale (perturbations of objects),* among other things.

2.7 Notes and Enhancements

1. SDM does not guarantee right answers any more than biological memories do.

2. Regardless of the extreme simplicity of the model -compared to human memory- , the retrieval properties, including the ways in which the memory fails, are lifelike.

3. The model captures some basic properties of long-term memory.

4. It can be used to build computer memory for very long words with approximate addressing.

5. Real data can be stored in SDM. In such a case, the critical distance and access radius will be real. An input cue will be matched against all hard locations to determine the ones within its access radius. Only those locations lying within the access radius will contribute to either read or write operations.

Chapter 3

SDM as a Feature-Matching Device

When reading from an SDM, what is retrieved in response to an input cue upon convergence is an average of all similar memory locations which contributed to the reading operation. So by storing variations of the Fourier descriptors -see chapter 4- of different vehicles in various forms (identity, scaled, rotated, translated) and matching an input image of a scene to those stored words, we can tell whether the input scene contains vehicles or not.

When writing into the SDM, the cue word is written into many locations which resemble that input cue.

When adding learning to future versions of TLCA, a new learned vehicle configuration can be enforced into the SDM by multiple writing. Thus representing enhanced or emotional memorization.

The KB (knowledge base) is pre-written into the SDM. All the entries in the knowledge base represent scenes including vehicles. The retrieval cue supplied to the SDM is matched with the closest, if any, stored pattern. Convergence in reading means that the image scene cued to the SDM has some match stored in the SDM. This in turn implies that the scene contains some vehicle(s) in it.

On the other hand, if divergence occurs in the reading operation in response to an input cue scene, this means that no vehicles were recognized in the scene. Hence no time slice of green light is needed for that direction.

The input cue in either case stands for a group of features of the input scene. More precisely, the Fourier Descriptors of the processed input image. Those descriptors can be modified easily to accommodate for scale, orientation, translation, and change of starting point. As a result, an input cue need not be the same as the stored ones. As a matter of fact, it can undergo scaling, orientation, or translation without affecting its correct recognition and classification.

Having the flexibility of the Fourier Descriptors in addition to the averaging effect of the SDM, gives us a robust recognition system to some extent.

The SDM used in TLCA is auto-associative, which means that a retrieval cue retrieves the closest match, if any, to itself.

The words in TLCA's SDM are made entirely from the Fourier descriptors of vehicle images. The action need not be stored since we have only two possible actions which are associated with convergence or divergence of the reading operation. Upon convergence of the reading operation, the direction is deemed active and the action is to give that direction a green time share. Upon divergence of the reading operation, the SDM may either consider the direction as passive and bypass its turn in green light, or it may send a feed back to the perception manager - see chapters 4,5- asking it to restart the interpretation of the scene at an earlier stage upto the sensation process. The criterion in which action to be taken upon divergence depends on how far the divergence was from the retrieval cue. If the divergence was oscillating in narrow range a little far from the critical distance, it might be reasonable to ask the perception manager to restart over its interpretation of the input scene hopping that the next interpretation will eliminate the divergence.

Chapter 4

Image Processing Techniques, Overview

In this chapter we will review some of the image processing fundamentals and techniques. Certainly, we will focus upon those techniques used and implemented in TLCA or those that will be needed to enhance TLCA according to the future directions (see chapter 8). The Digital Image Processing reference, Gonzalez and Woods (1993), on Image Processing is the primary source for this chapter. All the image processing techniques used in this project, are due, at least in-part, to John Reece.

4.1 Image Representation

A digital image is an image $f(x,y)$ that has been discretized both in spatial coordinates and in brightness or gray level -considering black and white images-. In the case of colored images, brightness is replaced by RGB, CMY, HSI, or any other color model; see Gonzalez and Woods (1993, sec 4.6), and Lindley (1991), for details.

A digital image can be considered a matrix whose row and column indices identify a point in the image, a pixel, and the corresponding matrix element value identifies the gray level at that point - considering black and white images only which is sufficient for the current version of TLCA-. See the figure below.

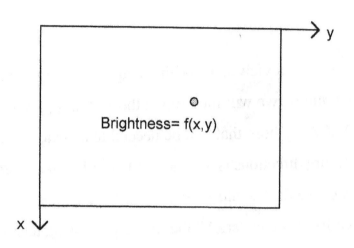

Fig 4.1-1 : Image Representation

4.2 Edge Detection

Edge detection is a process in which the edges of an object are outlined and/or extracted. In TLCA, we make use of one common technique of edge enhancement, namely the *Sobel* or gradient operators - see Gonzalez and Woods (1993, sec 7.1.3) for details- to process our input image pixel by pixel using a 3x3 mask. This process serves to emphasize changes in brightness or gray level values and to dim down areas with no change in gray level between their pixels, i.e., gradient technique.

The mask size determines how many neighbors of the current pixel are going to contribute in the enhancement operation. The 3x3 mask used in TLCA is depicted below:

$$
\begin{array}{ccc}
z1 & z2 & z3 \\
z4 & z5 & z6 \\
z7 & z8 & z9
\end{array}
$$

The masks used in TLCA are given below:

$$
\begin{array}{ccc}
-1 & -2 & -1 \\
0 & 0 & 0 \\
1 & 2 & 1
\end{array}
\qquad\qquad
\begin{array}{ccc}
-1 & 0 & 1 \\
-2 & 0 & 2 \\
-1 & 0 & 1
\end{array}
$$

$$G_X \qquad\qquad\qquad\qquad G_Y$$

where $G_X = (z_7 + 2z_8 + z_9) - (z_1 + 2z_2 + z_3)$

and $G_Y = (z_3 + 2z_6 + z_9) - (z_1 + 2z_4 + z_7)$

Adding G_X and G_Y in absolute value we obtain a good estimate of the gradient of the image in which the edges are enhanced and outlined much more than the original image. Thus:

edge detected image = gradient$(f(x,y)) = |G_X| + |G_Y|$

4.3 Thresholding

Thresholding is a process in which a digital image is converted into a binary image (on-off pixels). This is achieved by setting pixel values above certain threshold to a high or maximum gray level. Similarly, pixel values below the threshold are normally set to zero or background gray level. Having a binary image instead of a digital image serves to facilitate the manipulation and segmentation of the image. See Gonzalez and Woods (1993, sec 7.3) for more details.

Thresholding can be represented by the following simple function :

$$g(x,y) = \begin{array}{ll} 1 & \text{if } f(x,y) > \text{Threshold} \\ 0 & \text{if } f(x,y) < \text{Threshold} \end{array}$$

Where $f(x,y)$ is the original image and $g(x,y)$ is the binary image after thresholding.

4.4 Connectivity

Connectivity between pixels is an important concept used in establishing boundaries of objects and components of regions in an image. To determine whether two pixels are connected, it must be determined if they are adjacent in some sense (i.e. 4-neighbors or 8-neighbors) and if their gray levels satisfy a specified criterion of similarity (i.e. if they are equal. For example, in a binary image with values 0 and 1, two pixels, which are 4-neighbors, are not considered to be connected unless they have the same value. See Gonzalez and Woods (1993, sec 2.4.2 and sec 8.4.4).

4-neighborhood of a certain pixel considers the up, bottom, right, and left neighbors of the pixel, as depicted below:

$$
\begin{array}{ccc}
 & p & \\
p & Q & p \\
 & p & \\
\end{array}
$$

8-neighborhood of a certain pixel considers the 4-neighbors of the pixel in addition to the diagonal neighbors, as depicted below:

$$
\begin{array}{ccc}
p & p & p \\
p & Q & p \\
p & p & p \\
\end{array}
$$

4.5 Fourier Descriptors

The Fourier Descriptors of a group of image pixels are obtained by considering each pixel coordinates as a complex number :

$$s(k) = x(k) + j\, y(k)$$

The resulting set of complex numbers is then used as an input for DFT (Discrete Fourier Transform). See Gonzalez and Woods (1993, sec 8.2.3).

$$a(u) = DFT(\, s(k)\,)$$

The complex coefficients a(u) are called the Fourier Descriptors of the input set of points s(k) which may stand for a certain boundary.

One apparent advantage for such an approach is that it reduces the problem from 2-D to 1-D.

The Fourier Descriptors can be easily modified to accommodate for scale, rotation, translation, and change of starting point. This implies that they can be considered somehow invariant to such changes.

Chapter 5

Perception Modules in TLCA

In this chapter, we represent the current implemented modules for perception in TLCA. Those modules can be enhanced to improve the perceptual capability of TLCA. In addition the design is somehow flexible, thus allowing for the addition of further perceptual processing modules, e.g., motion detection or color recognition modules. Perception techniques were invoked from many references. See Kosslyn (1994), Kosslyn and Koenig (1992), Archibald and Kwok (1995), Haralick and Shapiro (1992), Zuech and Miller (1987), Leavers (1992), Neven, Steinhage, Giese, and Bruckhoff (1996), and Scheier and Lambrinos (1996), for details and discussions.

5.1 Layout

The diagram below depicts the current perception modules in TLCA along with their interactions:

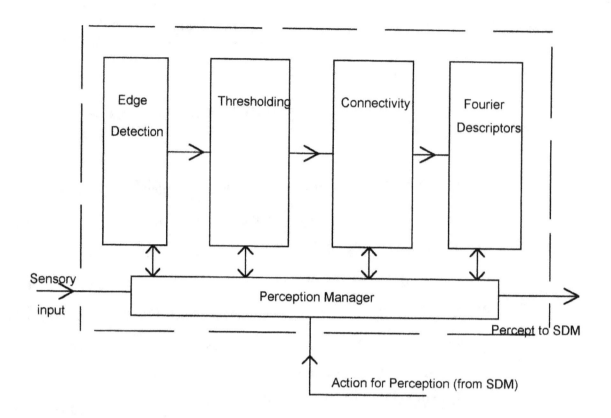

Fig 5.1-1 : The Perception Modules in TLCA

The Perception Manager performs two main functions :

1. controls the flow of the processed image between the different processing modules.

2. receives the feedback from the SDM and determines according to it where to restart the perception phase.

5.2 Edge Detection Module

The edge detection module uses the Sobel operators discussed in sec 4.2 to compute the gradient of the input image (sense). The output from the edge detection module is still an image but with the edge enhanced and outlined. Further processing of such an image to obtain representations of individual edges is straightforward and can be easily done.

The following schematic diagram represents the edge detection module:

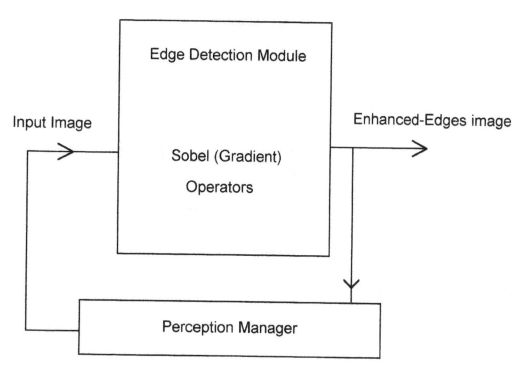

Fig 5.2-1 : Edge Detection Module in TLCA

5.3 Thresholding Module

After edge enhancement, the resulting gradient image should be thresholded to facilitate the work of the connectivity module (See sec 5.4). Thresholding is done straightforward as explained in sec 4.3.

The following schematic diagram represents the thresholding module:

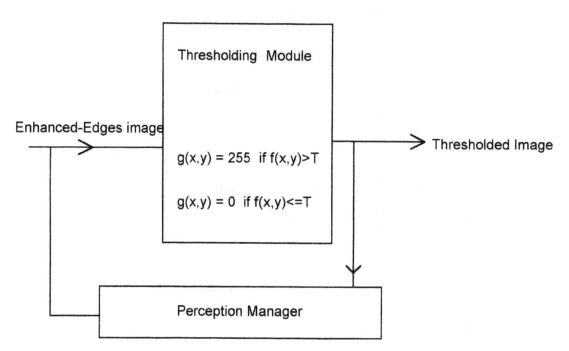

Fig 5.3-1 : Thresholding Module in TLCA

5.4 Connectivity Detection Module

The thresholded image produced in the previous phase, is then supplied to the connectivity module to discard isolated noise pixels and extract the connected components from the scene using the 4-neighborhood connectivity criterion. See sec 4.4 for details.

The following schematic diagram represents the connectivity detection module:

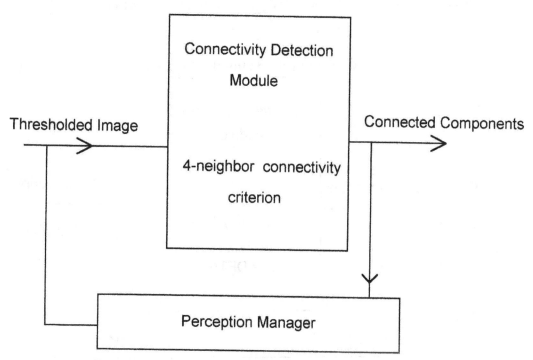

Fig 5.4-1 : Connectivity Detection Module in TLCA

5.5 Fourier Descriptors Module

The last phase in perception in TLCA involves extraction of the Fourier descriptors of each connected component in the image produced in the previous phase (by the connectivity module). Those descriptors, in turn, are supplied as an input vector of complex numbers to the SDM in order to determine whether the corresponding connected component can be classified as a vehicle or not. The process may be repeated for each connected component if an estimate of the number of vehicles is required. Alternatively, the process may stop as soon as any single vehicle is detected. The second alternative is what is followed in the current version of TLCA.

The following diagram represents the Fourier descriptors module:

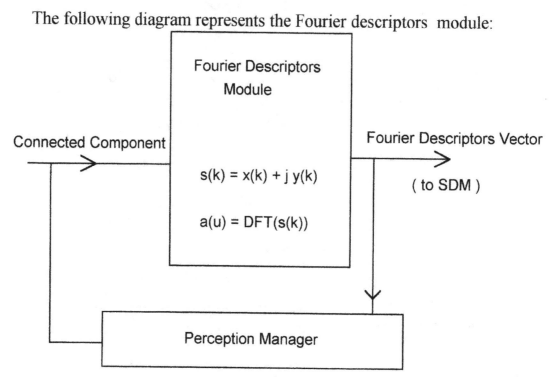

Fig 5.5-1 : Fourier Descriptors Module in TLCA

5.6 Perception Manager

The perception manager is responsible for controlling the navigation of the image form one phase to another in the perceptual apparatus. It may judge the value produced by each phase before passing it to the next phase according to some criteria. If the produced output does not meet such a criteria, the perception manager may ask the previous phase to reiterate its processing of the image. For example, if the output form the connectivity module includes too few connected components, e.g., one, the perception manager may ask the connectivity module to reprocess the thresholded image with different policy trying to obtain more connected components. If not successful, the perception manager might go a step further and ask the thresholding module to process the edge-detected image with a reduced value of the threshold.

The following schematic diagram represents the Perception Manager along with its interfaces with the various perceptual modules:

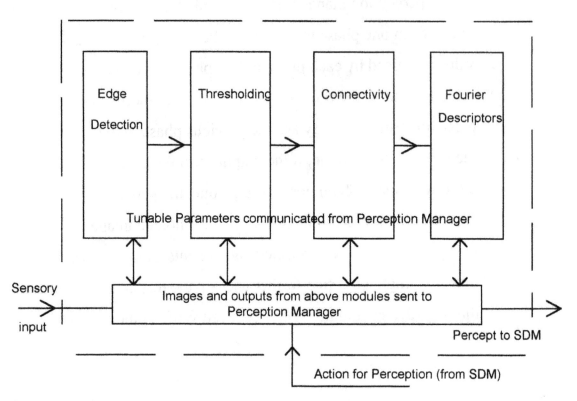

Fig 5.6-1 : The Perception Manager Interface

Chapter 6

TLCA in Operation

A complete cycle in the operation of TLCA follows :

1. The sensors from all directions in an intersection (cameras or other image-capturing device) send their images to TLCA.

2. TLCA takes those images one by one and passes them to the *Perception Manager,* see sec 6.1.

3. The perception manager keeps track of the image as it passes through the four perceptual processing phases (edge extraction, thresholding, connectivity detection, Fourier descriptors). A phase might be repeated if its output does not obey certain restrictions, e.g. the connectivity phase may be repeated to make the number of detected components above a certain minimum. The decision whether or not the output from a certain perception phase is satisfactory or not, is determined by a set of heuristics and metrics in the perception manager.

4. The vector containing the Fourier descriptors of a connected component is supplied as an input cue to the SDM.

5. The SDM goes into a read cycle to see whether a match exists for the input cue or not.

6. If a match exists, the direction corresponding to the input image is considered active and it becomes candidate for green light.

7. On the other hand, if no match exists, TLCA will either consider that direction passive and not a candidate for green light, or ask the perception manager to repeat some or all perception phases to get more dependable results (going back to step 3) as explained in chapter 3.

8. Steps 2 through 7 are repeated for each direction in the intersection.

9. Depending upon the state of each direction, active or passive, TLCA determines which direction to become green according to a quite simple control rule.

Chapter 7

Implementation, Results, Advantages and Drawbacks

The following is a short note about the current implementation of TLCA. An average run will take about 30 seconds on a slightly loaded 'Sun Sparc 4'.

7.1 Implementation

TLCA processing modules are written in ANSI C for sake of portability. The platform used is UNIX on Sun Solaris. Some packages for image viewing and conversion were used, e.g. xv and psp. Some of the code used in SDM modules is due in part to Stan Franklin. Also some of the code and libraries used in image processing and perception is due in part to John Reece.

7.2 Results

TLCA proved to be quite promising. Being able to recognize vehicles correctly in about 86% of the cases.

The images used for test were a mixture from day and night photographs of vehicles at intersections. The photographs were scanned and converted to *ras* format, then supplied as simulated input to TLCA.

Table 7.2-1 below summarizes the run results for TLCA:

Table 7.2-1 : Results

	Scenes with Vehicles	Scenes without Vehicles
Vehicle Existence Recognized	86%	4%
Vehicle Absence Recognized	14%	96%

As the table above shows, TLCA performs pretty well under regular circumstances.

7.3 Advantages

TLCA has many advantages over counterpart blind recognizers which might be used for the same task. Some of those advantages follow:

1. A blind sensor (mechanical or infra-red) is not able to detect contingencies, e.g., accidents or ambulance or police cars. Although not yet implemented in the current version, such enhancements can be added with moderate effort and they are among the future directions (see chapter 8, #1) to be considered.

2. TLCA has an advantage over such blind recognizers. With some extra work, TLCA will be able to determine estimates of number of vehicles in each

direction using the same modules and control mechanisms currently in use in addition to some new perception modules to be incorporated. On the other hand, to achieve this goal with blind sensors, a group of such sensors need to be used in each direction at distant intervals.

3. Another advantage TLCA has over blind sensors, is that an image can capture an incoming car from a long distance, whereas blind sensors cannot detect such a car unless planted upto a long distance from the intersection.

4. One more advantage of TLCA is that it can be centralized with the traffic light itself. The entire embodiment of TLCA can be a box smaller than the physical intersection light. On the other hand, using blind sensors will require implantation of sensors at regular distances, thus losing the advantage of a centralized control. In addition, extra expensive circuitry will be needed to transmit the signals from those remote blind sensors to the control circuitry governing the intersection.

7.4 Drawbacks

TLCA in its current condition relies on a separate external control device to supply the required input images. Integrating such a device with TLCA will make things better and smoother.

TLCA lacks color recognition capability which is needed for contingency handling.

Detection of motion is another aspect which TLCA lacks. It will be of use in future versions.

Chapter 8

Future Directions

Some of the possible enhancements to TLCA are summarized below. Most, if not all, of them will build mainly upon the existing modules and make use of them. I expect most of them to be added with a reasonable amount of effort.

The list of future directions and possible enhancements follows with order being somehow irrelevant :

1. Accommodation of contingencies, like accidents and ambulance or police cars in duty. Detection of smashed cars, red blood on the ground, and human bodies laid on the ground, will help in accident detection. Using the same or an additional SDM for accident templates, an input image may be classified as accident free or not. Detection of police cars and ambulances flashing their lights, i.e. in duty, needs extra work. The target to detect here is the flashing light of the vehicle.

2. Determination of number of vehicles in each direction which will help tune the duration of green light granted to each direction. Further perception modules are needed for this task. Dividing the input image into regions each of which denotes a part of a different vehicle. Accurate numbers will be hard to obtain but good estimates may be obtained, which is quite acceptable compared to the current traffic lights in use.

3. Adding learning capability to the agent. TLCA performance, which is already promising so far, can be enhanced by using in-field learning capability to tune the duration of green light granted to each direction depending on the number of vehicles in that direction.

4. Adding a physical hardware device, i.e. embodiment, see Franklin (1997), to the software agent will help make it a stand alone agent. Cameras to take pictures of the directions of an intersection need to be added along with some control circuitry and some storage for the SDM.

5. Detection of vehicle motion might help to differentiate between moving incoming cars versus parked cars on the road. Although a driver might prefer to keep his or her car stopped until the light becomes green, instead of approaching the lane center towards the intersection. In any event incorporation of movement detection may prove to be useful in differentiating between moving and stopped on-duty police cars or ambulances, which may help in determining the appropriate action for the contingency. A moving on-duty police car or ambulance needs green light, whereas a stopped one may be waiting for investigation or carrying injuries, or it may be in bad need of a green light.

6. TLCA may be a step in the long way to autonomous vehicles. The perception processing module in TLCA may well be used for approaching or surrounding vehicles recognition. See Neven, Steinhage, Giese, and Bruckhoff

(1996), and Schiere and Lambrinos (1996), for more discussion and references.

Chapter 9

Conclusion

- TLCA may be a step in the long way to autonomous vehicles.

- TLCA a step towards more efficient traffic lights

- Results are promising

- Even in simple domains, perception is needed after sensation

- SDM matches the percept with stored knowledge

- SDM in TLCA stands out as a successful control mechanism for action selection in autonomous agents.

- Physical implementation of TLCA needs special hardware

References

Albus, James S. (1981). *Brains, Behavior, and Robotics*. Byte Publications.

Albus, James S. (1991). *Outline for a Theory of Intelligence*.
IEEE Transactions on Systems, Man, and Cybernetics, vol 21 no. 3,
May/June.

Archibald, Colin, and Kwok, Paul. (1995). *Research in Computer and
Robot Vision*. World Scientific Publishing Co.

Baars, Bernard J. (1995). *A Cognitive Theory of Consciousness*. Cambridge
University Press.

Bates, Joseph, Loyall, Bryan, and Reilly, W. Scott. (1991). *Broad Agents*.
CMU.

Bates, Joseph, Loyall, Bryan, and Reilly, W. Scott. (1992). *An Architecture
for Action, Emotion, and Social Behavior*. CMU.

Boden, Margaret A. (1988). *Computer Models of Mind*. Cambridge
University Press.

Bundesen, Claus, and Shibuya, Hitomi. (1995). *Visual Selective Attention*.
Lawrence Erlbaum Associates Ltd.

Callari, Francesco G., and Ferrie, Frank P. (1996). *Active Recognition : Using Uncertainty to Reduce Ambiguity.* ICPR96.

Foner, Leonard N., and Maes, Pattie. (1994). *Paying Attention to What's Important.* Proceedings of SAB 94.

Franklin, Stan. (1995). *Artificial Minds.* MIT Press.

Franklin, Stan. (1997). *Autonomous Agents as Embodied AI.* Cybernetics and Systems, special issue on Epistemological Issues in Embedded AI.

Franklin, Stan, and Graesser, Art. (1997). *Is it an Agent, or just a Program? A Taxonomy for Autonomous Agents.* Proceedings of the Third International Workshop on Agent Theories, Architectures, and Languages, published as Intelligent Agents III, Springer-Verlag, 21-35.

Glenberg, Arthur M. (1997). What Memory is for? Behavioral and Brain Sciences.

Gonzalez, Rafael C., and Woods, Richard E. (1993). *Digital Image Processing.* Addison-Wesley.

Haralick, Robert M., and Shapiro, Linda G. (1992). *Computer and Robot Vision.* Addison-Wesley.

Kanerva, Pentti. (1990). *Sparse Distributed Memory.* MIT Press.

Karlsson, Roland. (1995). *Evaluation of a Fast Activation Mechanism for the Kanerva SDM.* RWCP Neuro SICS Laboratory.

Kosslyn, Stephen M. (1994). *Image and Brain.* MIT Press.

Kosslyn, Stephen M., and Koenig, Olivier. (1992). *Wet Mind.* Macmillan Inc.

Kristoferson, Jan. (1995a). *Some Comments on the Information Stored in SDM.* RWCP Neuro SICS Laboratory.

Kristoferson, Jan. (1995b). *Best Probability of Activation and Performance Comparisons for Several Designs of SDM.* RWCP Neuro SICS laboratory.

Leavers, V. F. (1992). *Shape Detection in Computer Vision Using the Hough Transform.* Springer-Verlag.

Lindley, Craig A. (1991). *Practical Image Processing in C.* John Wiley & Sons, Inc.

Neven, Hartmut, Steinhage, Axel, Giese, Martin, and Bruckhoff, Carsten.

(1996). *Dynamics for Vision-Based Autonomous Mobile Robots*. SAB 96 Proceedings.

Russell, Stuart, and Norvig, Peter. (1995). *Artificial Intelligence A Modern Approach*. Prentice-Hall Inc.

Scheier, Christian, and Lambrinos, Dimitrios. (1996). *Categorization in a Real-World Agent Using Haptic Exploration and Active Perception*. SAB 96 Proceedings.

Sjodin, Gunnar. (1995). *Convergence and New Operations in SDM*. RWCP Neuro SICS Laboratory.

Zuech, Nello, and Miller, Richard K. (1987). *Machine Vision*. The Fairmont Press.

www.ingramcontent.com/pod-product-compliance
Lightning Source LLC
Chambersburg PA
CBHW060203060326
40690CB00018B/4223